THE POWER

of

BOLD DECLARATION

"Thou shalt also decree a thing, and it shall be established unto thee: and the light shall shine upon thy ways."

Job22:28

by

Franklin N. Abazie

The power of bold declaration
COPYRIGHT 2019 *By* Franklin N Abazie
ISBN: 978:1-945-133-27-5

All right reserved. This book or any portion thereof may be reproduced or used in any manner whatsoever without the express written permission of the publisher, except for the use of brief quotations in a book review. All Bible quotes are from King James Version and others as noted.

Published by:
F N Abazie Publishing House-a.k.a,
Empowerment Bookstore:

That I may publish with the voice of thanksgiving and tell of all thy wondrous works.
Psalms 26:7

To order additional copies, wholesales or booking:
Call the Church office (973-372-7518)
or Empowerment Bookstore Hotline 973-393-8518

Worship address:
343 Sanford Avenue Newark New Jersey 07106
Administrative Head Office address:
33 Schley Street Newark New Jersey 07112
Email:pastorfranknto@yahoo.com
Website www.fnabaziehealingministries.org
Publishing House: www.fnabaziepublishinghouse.org

This book is a production of F N Abazie Publishing House. A publication Arms of Miracle of God Ministries 2019
First Edition

CONTENTS

The Mandate of The Commission iv

Favor Confession vi

Introduction viii

CHAPTER 1
The Power of The Spoken Word 37

CHAPTER 2
The Power of The Prophetic Word 62

CHAPTER 3
Prayer of Salvation 85

CHAPTER 4
About The Author 96

Books by Rev Franklin N Abazie 98

The Power of Bold Declaration

THE MANDATE OF THE COMMISSION

"THE MOMENT IS DUE TO IMPACT YOUR WORLD THROUGH THE REVIVAL OF THE HEALING & MIRACLE MINISTRY OF JESUS CHRIST OF NAZARETH."

"I AM SENDING YOU TO RESTORE HEALTH UNTO THEE AND I WILL HEAL THEE OF THY WOUNDS, SAID THE LORD OF HOST."

ARMS OF THE COMMISSION

1) F N Abazie Ministries-Miracle of God Ministries (Miracle Chapel Intl)
2) F N Abazie TV Ministries: Global Television Ministry Outreach.
3) F N Abazie Radio Ministries: Radio Broadcasting Outreach.
4) F N Abazie Publishing House: Book Publication.
5) F N Abazie Bible School: also called Word of Healing Bible School (W.O.H.B.S)
6) F N Abazie Evangelistic Ass: Miracle of God Ministries: Global Crusade
7) Empowerment Bookstore: Book distribution.
8) F N Abazie Helping Hands: Meeting the help of the needy world wide
9) F N Abazie Disaster Recovery Mission: Global Disaster Recovery.
10) F N Abazie Prison Ministry: Prison Ministry for all convicts "Second chance"

Some of our ministry arms are waiting the appointed time to commence.

The Power of Bold Declaration

FAVOR CONFESSION

Father thank you for making me righteous and accepted through the blood of Jesus Christ. Because of that, I am blessed and highly favored by God. I am the subject of your affection. Your favor surrounds me as a shield, and the first thing that people see around me is your favored shield.

Thank you that I have favor with you and man today. All day long people go out of their way to bless me and help me. I have favor with everyone that I deal with today. Doors that were once closed are now opened for me. I receive preferential treatment, and I have special privileges, I am Gods favored child.

No good thing will he withhold from me. Because of Gods favor my enemies cannot triumph over my life. I have supernatural increase and promotion. I declare restoration to everything that the devil has

Favor Confession

stolen from my life. I have honor in the midst of my adversaries and an increase in assets, especially in real estate and expansion of territories.

Because I am highly favored by God, I experience great victories, supernatural turnarounds, and miraculous breakthrough in the midst of great impossibilities. I receive recognition, prominence, and honor. Petitions are granted to me even by ungodly authorities. Policies, rules, regulations, and laws are changed and reverse on my behalf.

I win battles that I don't even have to fight, because God fights them for me. This is the day, the set time and the designated moment for me to experience the free favor of God, that profusely and lavishly abound on my behalf in Jesus name. **Amen.**

The Power of Bold Declaration

INTRODUCTION

"Thou shalt also decree a thing, and it shall be established unto thee: and the light shall shine upon thy ways." **Job22:28**

Every spoken word of faith is very powerful. As a student of faith, I have always believed God concerning –the spoken word. I have always believed in the power of God to create new things.

But I came to discover that until you speak out in faith, you cannot see it in reality. *Although the bible says, ...call those things that be not as if they are.* **Romans4:17** Often people mock and laugh at us when we make our bold confession. People look down on us when we declare boldly what we want to see in our desired future.

One great man said.......

"Flatter me, and I may not believe you. Criticize me, and I may not like you. Ignore me, and I may not forgive you. Encourage

Introduction

me, and I will not forget you. Love me and I may be forced to love you."— **William Arthur Ward.**

Bold declaration is the key into kingdom wealth. *"How forcible are right words! but what doth your arguing reprove?"* **Job 6:24.**

We must become conscious of every spoken word that comes out of our mouth.

"But I say unto you, That every idle word that men shall speak, they shall give account thereof in the day of judgment. For by thy words thou shalt be justified, and by thy words thou shalt be condemned." **Mathew 12:36-37**

Every word that you speak is a seed. It has power to create life and to produce frustration. *"Death and life are in the power of the tongue: and they that love it shall eat the fruit thereof."* **Proverb 18:21.**

Come with me let's examine what the Holy Spirit is saying in this book.

HIS DESTINY WAS THE CROSS....

HIS PURPOSE WAS LOVE....

HIS REASON WAS YOU....

"Whoever loves discipline loves knowledge, but he who hates reproof is stupid."

Proverb12:1

As many as I love, I rebuke and chasten: be zealous therefore, and repent.

Rev 3:19

> "I therefore so run, not as uncertainly; so fight I, not as one that beateth the air:"
> **1cor9:26**

"But I keep under my body, and bring it into subjection: lest that by any means, when I have preached to others, I myself should be a castaway."

1cor9:27

"I must work the works of him that sent me, while it is day: the night cometh, when no man can work."

John9:4

"Whoever spares the rod hates his son, but he who loves him is diligent to discipline him."

Proverb 13:24

"Those whom I love, I reprove and discipline, so be zealous and repent."
Revelation 3:19

"The rod and reproof give wisdom, but a child left to himself brings shame to his mother."

Proverb29:15

> "So he fed them according to the integrity of his heart; and guided them by the skilfulness of his hands."
>
> **Psalm 78:72**

"And ye have forgotten the exhortation which speaketh unto you as unto children, My son, despise not thou the chastening of the Lord, nor faint when thou art rebuked of him:"

Hebrews12:5

"For whom the Lord loveth he chasteneth, and scourgeth every son whom he receiveth."

Hebrews12:6

"If ye endure chastening, God dealeth with you as with sons; for what son is he whom the father chasteneth not"?

Hebrews 12:7

"But if ye be without chastisement, whereof all are partakers, then are ye bastards, and not sons."

Hebrews12:8

"Furthermore we have had fathers of our flesh which corrected us, and we gave them reverence: shall we not much rather be in subjection unto the Father of spirits, and live?"

Hebrews12:9

"He that spareth his rod hateth his son: but he that loveth him chasteneth him betimes."

Proverb13:24

> "Let thy work appear unto thy servants, and thy glory unto their children."
>
> **Psalm 90:16**

"And let the beauty of the Lord our God be upon us: and establish thou the work of our hands upon us; yea, the work of our hands establish thou it."

Psalm 90:17

"And he shall be like a tree planted by the rivers of water, that bringeth forth his fruit in his season; his leaf also shall not wither; and whatsoever he doeth shall prosper."

Psalm 1:3

"I must work the works of him that sent me, while it is day: the night cometh, when no man can work."

John9:4

"For even when we were with you, this we commanded you, that if any would not work, neither should he eat."
2theo3:10

xxx

"And that ye study to be quiet, and to do your own business, and to work with your own hands, as we commanded you;
1theo4:11

"To discipline a child produces wisdom, but a mother is disgraced by an undisciplined child."

Proverbs 29:15

"Whoever loves discipline loves knowledge, but whoever hates correction is stupid."

Proverbs 12:1

"Blessed is the one whom God corrects; so do not despise the discipline of the Almighty."

Job 5:17

"Blessed is the one you discipline, LORD, the one you teach from your law;"
Psalm 94:12

But Jesus answered them, My Father worketh hitherto, and I work.
John5:17

CHAPTER 1
THE POWER OF THE SPOKEN WORD

"Death and life are in the power of the tongue: and they that love it shall eat the fruit thereof."
Proverb 18:21

"How forcible are right words! but what doth your arguing reprove?" **Job 6:25**

"As the rain and the snow come down from heaven, and do not return to it without watering the earth and making it bud and flourish, so that it yields seed for the sower and bread for the eater, so is my word that goes out from my mouth: it will not return empty, but will accomplish what I desire and achieve the purpose for which I sent it."
Isaiah 55:10-11

"What? know ye not that your body is the temple of the Holy Ghost which is in you, which ye have of God, and ye are not your own? **1cor6:19**

We were told that the Holy Spirit dwells in us. *"For ye are bought with a price: therefore glorify God in your body, and in your spirit, which are God's."* **1cor6:20**

If the Holy Spirit dwells in us, therefore, He should speak through us. He gives us power to not only make decisions but also power to speak to our challenges, and obstacles in life.

"But if the Spirit of him that raised up Jesus from the dead dwell in you, he that raised up Christ from the dead shall also quicken your mortal bodies by his Spirit that dwelleth in you." **Romans8:11**

"For if ye live after the flesh, ye shall die: but if ye through the Spirit do mortify

Chapter 1 : The Power of The Spoken Word

the deeds of the body, ye shall live."
Romans8:13

Whenever we open our mouth to speak, our words has power and authority to build up or destroy any prevailing circumstance.

Here this…..

"Is not my word like as a fire? saith the Lord; and like a hammer that breaketh the rock in pieces?" **Jer23:29**

Every time we make bold declaration or confession, it is an *expression of our faith in Christ Jesus*. As believers whenever you make a positive confession, it becomes a decree that must be established within a time frame.
(See **Job22:29**)

In the same manner, whenever we make a negative confession it establishes fear-that encourages the devil to enforce his wicked task against our life. Negative words gives the enemy advantage to afflict us in life.

Job made such a statement and he suffered severely. *"For the thing which I greatly feared is come upon me, and that which I was afraid of is come unto me. I was not in safety, neither had I rest, neither was I quiet; yet trouble came."* **Job3:25-26**

On the contrary, if you declare the blessings of God, you activate it by your spoken word. Solomon said, "…you have been trapped by what you said, ensnared by the words of your mouth" (Proverbs 6:2).

There is no idle word in the kingdom. Every declaration you make reflects upon your life, whether it is positive confession or a negative word. I pray you learnt to practice speaking the right word at all time.

Say this after me……….

Chapter 1 : The Power of The Spoken Word

Say I am the head and not the tail. A winner, and not a beggar. I am on top and not beneath. I am blessed and not cursed. I am rich and not poor in Jesus Mighty Name Amen

There is a mystery about *every spoken word* that we *speak in life*. Every *spoken word* has *power to create* and to *destroy in life*. Jesus said there is no idle word in the kingdom. **"What you say is what you shall have in life".**

Every time you speak, you influence your world, and affects future. You are either building it up or tearing it down.

"But I say unto you, That every idle word that men shall speak, they shall give account thereof in the day of judgment. For by thy words thou shalt be justified, and by thy words thou shalt be condemned." **Mathew 12:36-37**

The word is healing and medicinal, as long as you speak it by faith. *"He sent his word, and healed them, and delivered them from their destructions."* **Psalm107:20**

"My son, attend to my words; incline thine ear unto my sayings. Let them not depart from thine eyes; keep them in the midst of thine heart. For they are life unto those that find them, and health to all their flesh." **Proverb4:20-22**

Our tongue is powerful. *If you always confess, blessing in life, you will witness the blessing of God in life.* If you confess sickness, disease, and lack in life, you shall see lack, sickness, and disease in your life.

WE MUST SPEAK THE RIGHT WORD IN ALL SITUATION

"Therefore I take pleasure in infirmities, in reproaches, in necessities, in persecutions, in distresses for Christ's sake:

Chapter 1 : The Power of The Spoken Word

for when I am weak, then am I strong." **2Cor12:10**

"Beat your plowshares into swords and your pruninghooks into spears: let the weak say, I am strong." **Joel 3:10**

"Say ye to the righteous, that it shall be well with him: for they shall eat the fruit of their doings." **Isaiah3:10**

We must therefore control what we say with our tongue in life.

"And the tongue is a fire, a world of iniquity: so is the tongue among our members, that it defileth the whole body, and setteth on fire the course of nature; and it is set on fire of hell." **James3:6**

"But the tongue can no man tame; it is an unruly evil, full of deadly poison." **James3:8**

"Suffer not thy mouth to cause thy flesh to sin; neither say thou before the angel, that it was an error: wherefore should God be angry at thy voice, and destroy the work of thine hands?" **Eccl5:6**

But what saith it? The word is nigh thee, even in thy mouth, and in thy heart: that is, the word of faith, which we preach; **Romans10:8**

"We having the same spirit of faith, according as it is written, I believed, and therefore have I spoken; we also believe, and therefore speak;" **2cor4:13**

It is important to be conscious of the word we speak daily. Some people talk negatively even in their dreams. *What you say is what you will get.* There is no two ways about it in life. *"For where your treasure is, there will your heart be also."* **Mathew6:21**

We must be conscious of what we say in our trials, in time of tribulation, and in time of pleasure. A rich fool said the wrong word

Chapter 1 : The Power of The Spoken Word

and the same day He died of heart attack in the bible.

THE RICH FOOL'S SPOKEN WORD THAT KILLED HIM

"And I will say to my soul, Soul, thou hast much goods laid up for many years; take thine ease, eat, drink, and be merry. But God said unto him, Thou fool, this night thy soul shall be required of thee: then whose shall those things be, which thou hast provided?" **Luke12:19-20**

NEBUCHADNEZZAR SPOKEN WORD THAT DESTROYED HIM

"The king spake, and said, Is not this great Babylon, that I have built for the house of the kingdom by the might of my power, and for the honour of my majesty? While the word was in the king's mouth, there fell a voice from heaven, saying, O king Nebuchadnezzar, to thee it is spoken;

The kingdom is departed from thee." **Daniel 4:30-31**

WE ARE COMMANDED….

"Delight thyself also in the Lord: and he shall give thee the desires of thine heart." **Psalm37:4**

"For where your treasure is, there will your heart be also." **Mathew6:21**

Whatever you want to see in life, you must confess it with your mouth. For unless you say, *no weapon fashioned against me shall prosper*, you are subject to the attack of the devil.

"No weapon that is formed against thee shall prosper; and every tongue that shall rise against thee in judgment thou shalt condemn. This is the heritage of the servants of the Lord, and their righteousness is of me, saith the Lord." **Isaiah54:17**

Chapter 1 : The Power of The Spoken Word

YOU SHALL HAVE WHATSOEVER YOU SAY

The power of bold declaration means; you must speak what you want to see in life. *You are only entitled to what you say in life.*

"For verily I say unto you, That whosoever shall say unto this mountain, Be thou removed, and be thou cast into the sea; and shall not doubt in his heart, but shall believe that those things which he saith shall come to pass; he shall have whatsoever he saith." **Mark11:23**

"The wicked is snared by the transgression of his lips: but the just shall come out of trouble." **Proverb12:14**

"Thou art snared with the words of thy mouth, thou art taken with the words of thy mouth." **Proverb6:2**

The Power of Bold Declaration

RENEW YOUR MIND

"And be not conformed to this world: but be ye transformed by the renewing of your mind, that ye may prove what is that good, and acceptable, and perfect, will of God." **Romans12:2**

I encourage you therefore to renew your mind, through the power of the words that you speak daily.

Listen to me....

The word we speak daily they are spirit, and they are life.

Here this……

"It is the spirit that quickeneth; the flesh profiteth nothing: the words that I speak unto you, they are spirit, and they are life." **John6:63**

Perhaps you said something and someone says to you, *"You are going to*

Chapter 1 : The Power of The Spoken Word

eat those words". It may sound like a mere phrase to you, but in reality we do eat our words. What we say not only affects our family, others, but it also affects and impacts on our future.

Spoken words are powerful and authoritative, especially when spoken and directed to the right circumstance. The spoken right word reprograms our mind. It gives us confidence to pursue our desired future. *"A man hath joy by the answer of his mouth: and a word spoken in due season, how good is it!"* **Proverb15:23**

We can literally increase our joy by speaking right words. We can also destroy our selves and others, by our negative confession.

What Happens When We Speak?

Spiritual things are higher than physical things in life. Whenever we speak in the

physical, *we speak in the spirit. Because spoken words cannot be seen. It can only be heard.* Therefore spoken words are spiritual. *"For it is not ye that speak, but the Spirit of your Father which speaketh in you".*
Mathew 10:20

Your words design your future. *You are either building a great future, or you are destroying a great future.* The words that come out of our mouth goes into our own ears as well as the ears of other hearers. Although *everyone's interpretation is different,* for the most part, negative words has power to re-program the mind. "For as he thinketh in his heart, so is he: Eat and drink, saith he to thee; but his heart is not with thee."
Proverb 23:7

I have often said, "Where the mind goes, the man follows". And it could also be said that where the mind goes, the mouth follows!

Chapter 1 : The Power of The Spoken Word

How does the Power of our Spoken Words affect others?

If we agree that words spoken to us have the capacity or power to affect the way we feel about ourselves, others and our world, then we must agree also, that the same words have the potential to impact all those around us. we can hurt or we can heal our lives and people around us. *The choice is ours, every time we open our mouth to speak.*

Using the Power of Spoken Words to Heal.

"My son, attend to my words; incline thine ear unto my sayings. Let them not depart from thine eyes; keep them in the midst of thine heart. For they are life unto those that find them, and health to all their flesh." **Proverb 4:20-22**

The Power of Bold Declaration

"He sent his word, and healed them, and delivered them from their destructions." **Psalm 107:20**

The power of spoken words is a fundamental building block to many self-help as well as main stream therapies. Most Physicians, spiritualist healer, psychologist, psychiatrists. Etc., all use the power of the spoken word to heal in their discipline.

For what we say out loud is a guide to what lies within us. If our talk is critical, cynical, or destructive, then we tend to think about ourselves in a similar way. *What you say is what you behave.*

Quite simply, there is power in what you think, and in what you say. When we don't like or approve of much others, we tend to talk down on it. Beware!! Those word always come back to haunt us in life.

The power of positive thinking has been well documented. Change the way you

Chapter 1 : The Power of The Spoken Word

think or talk to yourself and you will change yourself. The words you speak to yourself in the privacy of your mind have power too. This sounds too simple to be true, doesn't it? But it is.

Shakespeare said it like this: 'Nothing is either good or bad.' Tis thinking makes it so.' Words create our world.

We must practice speaking the right word always

To speak the right word at all time, is a habit. And they say it takes thirty days to form a habit. It is not an easy task to practice speaking the right word every time. *Speaking the right word, is something we must routinely practice until the habit is formed.* It is beneficial if you are accustomed to speaking the right word at all time. The devil will have no opportunity to afflict your life.

The Power of Bold Declaration

BE CONSCIOUS OF THE RIGHT WORD

I am not suggesting for you to deny the reality, but we must be conscious of whatever comes out of our mouth. *I do not want you to be ignorant also of the truth* either. In life, we are already faced with multiple challenges, obstacles, and financial limitation, sickness and disease. *The least any believer can do is to speak life to any challenging situation, speak health to any sick condition. Speak strength to any weak condition.* The bible says "…. *let the weak say, I am strong."* **Joel 3:10**

What are we saying?

I believe if we can practice saying those things we confess in prayers. If you can speak daily all those right positive things you ask God in prayers the devil will not have a chance in your life.

Chapter 1 : The Power of The Spoken Word

HOW TO LIVE A LIFE FULL OF JOY

Whom having not seen, ye love; in whom, though now ye see him not, yet believing, ye rejoice with joy unspeakable and full of glory:

"A merry heart doeth good like a medicine: but a broken spirit drieth the bones." **Proverb17:22**

"The spirit of a man will sustain his infirmity; but a wounded spirit who can bear?" **Proverb18:14**

Our words play a great role in shaping our lives and destiny. Whatever we say daily has power to design our future. Every time we speak, we are either building a great future or destroying a great future.

Often times, most of our problem is a decision issue, or lack of relevant information. Our spoken word is not totally responsible for all our problems. But they contribute ninety five percent to our present state. Our words play a great role in our life. One thing is certain, speaking negative words-will always hurt you while speaking positive words will always blesses our lives.

If you must get the most of life, you must embrace speaking the right word against any odd, or prevailing situation facing your life.

"Thou wilt shew me the path of life: in thy presence is fulness of joy; at thy right hand there are pleasures for evermore." **Psalm16:11**

"Therefore with joy shall ye draw water out of the wells of salvation." Isaiah12:3

The Holy Spirit is within us. Therefore if you must be joyful everyday of your life, you must appreciate the mystery of thanksgiving. Always appreciate God, and be thankful in life. What has happen we

Chapter 1 : The Power of The Spoken Word

know, what would have happen we do not know. Therefore thank God for life at all time.

We must make God the center of our living. If we must get the most joy in our life. We must speak the right word even in the face of trials, tribulation, or death.

"Nay, in all these things we are more than conquerors through him that loved us. For I am persuaded, that neither death, nor life, nor angels, nor principalities, nor powers, nor things present, nor things to come, Nor height, nor depth, nor any other creature, shall be able to separate us from the love of God, which is in Christ Jesus our Lord." **Romans8:37-39**

Your breakthrough is in mouth.

"I am the Lord thy God, which brought thee out of the land of Egypt: open thy mouth wide, and I will fill it." **Psalm81:10**

The Power of Bold Declaration

Your future is in your mouth speak it out.

"For I will give you a mouth and wisdom, which all your adversaries shall not be able to gainsay nor resist." **Luke21:15**

There is supernatural power in the things we say daily. I commend you to rise up and speak up. You must take advantage of your future by speak the right word.

The power of the spoken word is a concept shared by many cultures and its roots go deep into pre-literate history. The most widely cited written reference in western civilization comes from the Bible.

YOU ARE IN SPIRITUAL CAPTIVITY BY THE WAY YOU THINK

Although our thoughts are powerful, the spoken word is even more powerful. We must change the way we think, especially

Chapter 1 : The Power of The Spoken Word

before we speak out any word. *"Thou art snared with the words of thy mouth, thou art taken with the words of thy mouth."* **Proverb6:2**

"For as he thinketh in his heart, so is he: Eat and drink, saith he to thee; but his heart is not with thee." **Proverb23:7**

"A good man out of the good treasure of his heart bringeth forth that which is good; and an evil man out of the evil treasure of his heart bringeth forth that which is evil: for of the abundance of the heart his mouth speaketh" **Luke6:45**

"And he said, That which cometh out of the man, that defileth the man. For from within, out of the heart of men, proceed evil thoughts, adulteries, fornications, murders, Thefts, covetousness, wickedness, deceit, lasciviousness, an evil eye, blasphemy, pride, foolishness: All these evil things come from within, and defile the man." **Mark 7:20-23**

In summary:

1) *We must take heed of the words you speak at all time.*

2) *We must always think and reason before we speak out.*

3) *Never judge a matter by one person's statement.*

4) *Always pay attention to what God wants you to say or to do.*

5) *Always speak in faith what you expect to happen in your life.*

6) *Never let anyone's opinion influence your life and your own opinion.*

7) *Always remain positive in the face of adversaries and prevailing challenges in life.*

Chapter 1 : The Power of The Spoken Word

8) *Always believe God that your breakthrough day is coming.*

9) *Never give up in life. Strive for excellence and be the best in what you do.*

10) *Always be a blessing to someone less privilege.*

CHAPTER 2

THE POWER OF THE PROPHETIC WORD

"..but he that prophesieth edifieth the church".
1cor14:4

The prophetic word is powerful! Prophecy is an old tradition. It is the gift from God that balances the revelatory office of a minister. I believe every minister should operate in the prophetic. Despite all the criticism, and abuse of the prophetic, we desperately need the prophetic in this end time.

"For I am the Lord: I will speak, and the word that I shall speak shall come to pass; it shall be no more prolonged: for in your days, O rebellious house, will I say

Chapter 2 : The Power of The Prophetic Word

the word, and will perform it, saith the Lord God." **Ezekiel12:25**

"Therefore say unto them, Thus saith the Lord God; There shall none of my words be prolonged any more, but the word which I have spoken shall be done, saith the Lord God." **Ezekiel12:28**

For ages now, the prophetic office has come under great scrutiny and criticism. Some unqualified men have made merchandize of this office. The prophetic must be pure, and sanctified. Often some fellows speak as led by their emotions and not of God.

"Who is he that saith, and it cometh to pass, when the Lord commandeth it not?"
Lamentation3:37

Although *prophecy must be judged, prophetic words are comforting, encouraging, exalting, and edifying.*

The Power of Bold Declaration

God speaks to us in prophecy to give us revelation, warning about what is about to happen in our life. *"But he that prophesieth speaketh unto men to edification, and exhortation, and comfort."* **1cor14:3**

"This charge I commit unto thee, son Timothy, according to the prophecies which went before on thee, that thou by them mightest war a good warfare;" **1timothy1:18**

God spoke about you from the day you were born. There is a prophecy over your life that must be fulfilled in your life time.

"Son of man, I have made thee a watchman unto the house of Israel: therefore hear the word at my mouth, and give them warning from me." **Ezekiel3:17**

The word of God in your mouth is powerful and forceful. *Whatever you say is what you will see in your life time.* I

Chapter 2 : The Power of The Prophetic Word

therefore urge you to always speak the word of life. Always be conscious of anything that you say in life

Never neglect the power of the prophetic word of God in your mouth.

Remember… The spirit of a prophet is subject to the prophet.

"And the spirits of the prophets are subject to the prophets." **1cor14:32.** We must be conscious of the word we speak at all times, especially under the prophetic.

There is power in every word that you speak. Even in your dream.

You may say a word today, but it may take more than ten years for that prophetic word to come to pass. Therefore we must be ready to take advantage of the prophetic word of God on our lips and upon our life.

The prophetic word about Sarah took twenty five years to come to pass

"And he said, I will certainly return unto thee according to the time of life; and, lo, Sarah thy wife shall have a son. And Sarah heard it in the tent door, which was behind him." **Genesis18:10**

"And the Lord said unto Abraham, Wherefore did Sarah laugh, saying, Shall I of a surety bear a child, which am old?" **Genesis18:13**

"And the Lord visited Sarah as he had said, and the Lord did unto Sarah as he had spoken." **Genesis21:1**

"For Sarah conceived, and bare Abraham a son in his old age, at the set time of which God had spoken to him." **Genesis21:2**

"To another the working of miracles; to another prophecy; to another discerning of spirits; to another divers kinds of tongues; to another the interpretation of tongues:" **1cor12:10**

Chapter 2 : The Power of The Prophetic Word

God speak through us.

Jesus said there is no idle word in the kingdom of God. We must be conscious of the word we speak at all time. There is a strange power in the prophetic word we speak.

THE POWER OF THE CREATIVE WORD

Heaven and Earth *was created by the creative word of God*. Every word that we speak has power to create.

"By the word of the Lord the heavens were made, their starry host by the breath of his mouth." **Psalm33:6**

"For he spoke, and it came to be; he commanded, and it stood firm." **Psalm33:9**

The creative word in your mouth has power to create a great future for us.

HINDRANCE TO THE PROPOHETIC WORD

-----Negative mindset---

"And be renewed in the spirit of your mind;" **Ephesians 4:23**

For unless we change the way we think, we will miss the blessing of our prophetic word.

-------Doubt......

Every time we doubt we make the word of God ineffective in our lives. If you must doubt, doubt yourself. Never doubt God. *"A double minded man is unstable in all his ways."*

1) THE BLESSING OF THE PROPHETIC WORD

---------Awareness

Whenever you speak the prophetic word in advance, you take advantage of

Chapter 2 : The Power of The Prophetic Word

your future. The prophetic word has power to change any demonic event programed against your life. It is good to be aware of what is about to happen. It is even awesome to speak out the prophetic word and reverse the plan of the devil.

LONG LIFE

Longevity is a product of the spoken prophetic word. *"I shall not die, but live, and declare the works of the Lord."* **Psalm118:17**

GOOD HEALTH

The prophetic word is health to our flesh. The bible says the prophetic word is good health if you are conscious of it.

"For they are life unto those that find them, and health to all their flesh." **Proverb4:22**

DIVINE WISDOM

"For I will give you a mouth and wisdom, which all your adversaries shall not be able to gainsay nor resist." **Luke21:15**

The prophetic word is advance knowledge. If you know ahead and see ahead, you will move ahead. Divine wisdom is power, it is stability and progressive. *"But the path of the just is as the shining light, that shineth more and more unto the perfect day."* **Prover4:18**

DAILY STRENGTH

The right word give us daily strength. If you speak positively daily you will remain strong in the face of prevailing circumstances. Speak the right word daily and watch God transform your life.

Chapter 2 : The Power of The Prophetic Word

CONCLUSION

"Thou shalt also decree a thing, and it shall be established unto thee: and the light shall shine upon thy ways". **Job22:28**

"…….for of the abundance of the heart his mouth speaketh.." **Luke6:45**

"Therefore if any man be in Christ, he is a new creature: old things are passed away; behold, all things are become new". **2cor5:17**

I encourage you to repent in prayers of any negative word you have ever spoken against your life and future. Speak the right word and make these confessions boldly in faith.

REPEAT THIS PRAYER AFTER ME….

"Say Lord Jesus, I accept you today, as my Lord and my savior, forgive me of my

sins wash me with your blood. Right now, I believe, I am sanctified. I am save. I am free. I am free from the Power of sin to serve the Lord Jesus. Thank you Lord for saving me. **Amen**.*"*

What must I do to determine my divine visitation?

To determine divine visitation you must be born again! *The word says as many as received him, to them gave He power to become the sons of God. Even to them that believe on his name.*

To qualify for divine visitation do the following sincerely

1) Acknowledge that you are a sinner and that He died for you.Rom3:23.

2) Repent of your sins. Acts 3:19, Luke13:5, 2Peter3:9

3) Believe in your heart that Jesus died for your sin.Romans10:10

Chapter 2 : The Power of The Prophetic Word

4) Confess Jesus as the Lord over your life. Romans10:10, Acts2:21

I really want to hear from you. You can join me if you are in the area to worship with us

MIRACLE OF GOD MINISTRIES INC

343 SANFORD AVENUE NEWARK
NEW JERSEY 07106
Jesus is Lord!

EMAIL: Pastorfranknto@yahoo.com
Website www.fnabaziehealingministries.org

Please feel free to write me

REV FRANKLIN N ABAZIE
33 Schley street Newark
New Jersey 07112

Chapter 2 : The Power of The Prophetic Word

WISDOM KEYS

Every Productive Society is a society heading to the top

Millions of Nigerians run away from Nigeria, very few Nigerians stay in Nigeria.

My decision to return Nigeria is the will of God for my life

My short coming in America after 18 years, trained me to be wise, to think, reflect and reason appropriately.

If you train your mind to reason it will train your hands to earn money.

It is absurd to use the money of the heathen to build the kingdom of the living God.

Every Ministry reveals its agenda and goal either at the beginning or at the end. Be careful of your life it is your first Ministry.

The average American mind is conditioned for a continual quest to get new things and (discard the former) and throw away old things.

When I considered well, my BMW jeep became my initial deposit for the work of the ministry in Nigeria

Everyone is waiting for you to change your mind until you change your thinking nothing changes around you.

Multiple academic degrees in other discipline gave me the chance to think, reflect, and reason

What so everyone are thinking and reflecting at the moment reveals you to the time and the now factor

All events and intents are the product of precise thought processes, accurate reason every event is designed for a designated timeline

Chapter 2 : The Power of The Prophetic Word

Wisdom is your ability to think, to create and invent. If you can think wise enough you will come out of penury

The distance between you and success is your creative ability to think reason and reflect accurate.

Success is the result of hard work, commitment resolve, and determination, learning from past mistakes and failing.

If you organize your mind you have organized your life and destiny.

There is a thin line between success and failure. If you look above and beyond you are on your way to success.

Wealth is your ability to think, power is your ability to reason and success is your ability to be informed.

If you can make use of your mind by thinking and reasoning God will make use of your life and destiny.

The Power of Bold Declaration

Think and Be Great

Reflect, Reason, think and be great

Famous people are born of woman

That you will make it is your intention; that you will survive is your resolve, that you will succeed with changes is your determination, personal efforts and hard work.

No man was born a failure. Lack of vision is the end product of failure.

Working with mental patients encourages and aspire me to be a productive observant and dedicated to my assignment.

Successful people are not magicians, it is the will power combined with hard work, and determination and a resolve to succeed that make them succeed.

In the unequivocal state of the mind, intention is not a location or a position it is the state of the mind.

Chapter 2 : The Power of The Prophetic Word

So many people think that they think. The mind is used to think reflect and reason. You will remain blind with your eye open until you can see with your mind by thinking.

There is no favoritism in accurate and precise calculation

Although knowledge is power, information is the key and gateway to a great future.

It will take the hand of God to move the hand of man.

With the backing of the great wise God, nothing will disconnect you from your inheritance.

As long as you have wisdom and understanding of God, Satan and evil cannot manipulate your life and destiny.

You have come this far by yourself judgment and decision you have made in the past, now lean and listen to God for another dimension of greatness.

The Power of Bold Declaration

Great people are common people it is extra ordinary effort and the price of sacrifice that produces greatness.

As a mental direct care worker I saw a great pastor and a motivational speaker within myself.

Menial job does not reduce your self-worth, until you resolve to achieve greatness see greatness in all you do; you will never count in your community.

The principle of Jesus will solve your gambling and addiction problems

The man of Jesus will lead you into heaven,

Everyone have their self-appraisal and what they think about you. Until you discover yourself other opinion about you will alter the real you.

Supervisors and directors are just a position in the chain of command in a work place.

Chapter 2 : The Power of The Prophetic Word

Never allow your supervisor hierarchy to alter your opinion about yourself.

Everyone can come out of debt if they make up their mind.

That I am not a decision maker at work does not diminish my contribution to my world.

Although it appears like it was a poor decision to accept a direct care employment at a psychiatric hospital as I reflect of my nine years of experience, it became apparent that I have learnt and experienced enough for my next assignment.

Self-encouragement and determination is a resolve of the heart.

If you are determined to make a difference, and do the things that make a difference you will eventually make a difference.

Good things do not come easy

Short cuts will cut your life short.

The Power of Bold Declaration

Those who look ahead move ahead.

Life is all about making an impact. In your life time strive to make an impact in your community.

Make friends and connect with people who are moving ahead of you in life.

If you can look around well you have come a long way in your life, made a lot of difference and realized a lot of success in life.

If you are my old friend, hurry up to reach out to me before I become a stranger to you.

Everything I am blessed with inspirations from God, that change my definition and interpretation of the world around me.

I thought I was stagnant and lonely until I looked around and noticed my children running around and my wife cooking.

At 40 I resigned my Job to seek the Lord forever.

Chapter 2 : The Power of The Prophetic Word

My ministry took a drastic rise to the top when the wisdom of God visited me with knowledge and understanding.

You will be a better person if you understand the characteristics of your personality – your mood swings attitudes and habits.

It is the seed of love you sow into the heart of a child and a woman that you reap in due time.

Love is not selfish, love share everything including the concealed secrets of the mind.

As long as you have a prayer life and a bible; you will never feel lonely, rejected, and idle in the race of life.

When good friends disconnect from you, let them go, they might have seen something new in a different direction.

Confidence in yourself and in God is the only way to bring you out of captivity

Never train a child to waste his/her time.

The Power of Bold Declaration

The mind is the greatest assets of a great future.

You walk by common sense run by principles and fly by instruction.

CHAPTER 3
PRAYER OF SALVATION

"Neither is there salvation in any other: for there is none other name under heaven given among men, whereby we must be saved."

Acts 4:12

There is only one name that will take us into heaven.

What must I do to determine my salvation?

To be saved we must be born again! The word says as many as received him, to them gave He power to become the sons of God. Even to them that believe on his name.

To qualify for divine visitation do the following sincerely

The Power of Bold Declaration

1) Acknowledge that you are a sinner and that He died for you. Rom3:23.

2) Repent of your sins. Acts 3:19, Luke13:5, 2Peter3:9

3) Believe in your heart that Jesus died for your sin. Romans10:10

4) Confess Jesus as the Lord over your life. Romans10:10, Acts2:21

Are you saved?

If God have saved your life, speak to someone about Jesus. Disciple someone to join you worship the Lord Jesus Christ.

MIRACLE CARE OUTREACH

"…But that the members should have the same care one for another" 1cor12:25

We are all members of the body of Christ. Jesus commanded us to love our

Chapter 3 : Prayer of Salvation

neighbor as ourselves. This includes caring for one another as a member of one body. True love is expressed in caring and giving. The word says for God so Love He gave….

Reach out to someone in need of Jesus, help someone in crisis find Christ. Look out and prove your love to Jesus by caring and inviting your friends and associates to find Jesus the Healer.

Invite your friends to our Home Care Cell Fellowship (Miracle chapel Intl Satellite fellowship) In the USA at 33 Schley Street Newark New Jersey 07112.

If you are in Nigeria—**MIRACLE OF GOD MINISTRIES**

A.K.A"**MIRACLE CHAPEL INTL"** Mpama –Egbu-Owerri Imo state Nigeria.

(Home Care Cell fellowship Group).We meet every Tuesday at 6:00pm-7:00pm.

LIFE IS NOT ALL ABOUT DURATION BUT ITS ALL ABOUT DONATION

What does the above statement mean?....

Life consists not in accumulation of material wealth. (Luke12:15) But it's all about liberality....meaning- what you can give and share with others. Proverb11:25. When you live for others--You live forever-because you out live your generation by the legacy you live behind after you depart into glory to be with the Lord. But when you live to yourself - you are reduced to self—you are easily forgotten when you die and depart in glory. Permit me to admonish you today to live your life to be a blessing to a soul connected to you today. I want you to know that so many souls are connected and looking up to you, and through you so many souls will be saved and rescued from

Chapter 3 : Prayer of Salvation

destruction. Will you disciple someone today to find Jesus Christ?

As a genuine Christian; it is your duty to evangelize Jesus Christ to all you meet on your way. Jesus is still in the healing business-Jesus is still doing miracles from time of old to now. Therefore tell someone about Jesus Christ today, disciple and bring them to Church. John 1:45 *Philip findeth Nathanael....*

Please to prove the sincerity of your love for God today; please become a soul winner. The dignity of your Christianity is hidden in your boldness to proclaim and evangelize Jesus Christ to all you meet on your way. There is a question mark on the integrity of your Christianity until you become a life soul winner. Invite someone to join us worship the Lord Jesus this coming Sunday. **Amen**

MIRACLE OF GOD MINISTRIES PILLARS OF THE COMMISSION

We Believe Preach and Practice the following

1) We believe and preach Salvation to every living human being
2) We believe and preach Repentance and forgiveness of sins
3) We believe and preach the baptism of the Holy Spirit and Spiritual gifts
4) We believe and teach the Prosperity
5) We believe and preach Divine Healing and Miracles (Signs &Wonder)
6) We believe and preach Faith
7) We believe and Proclaim the Power of God (Supernatural)
8) We believe and Proclaim Praise& Worship to God

Chapter 3 : Prayer of Salvation

9) We believe and preach Wisdom
10) We believe and preach Holiness (Consecration)
11) We believe and preach Vision
12) We believe and teach the Word of God
13) We believe and teach Success
14) We believe and practice Prayer
15) We believe and teach Deliverance

This 15 stones form the Pillars of Our Commission. Become part of this church family and follow this great move of God.

MY HEART FELT PRAYER FOR YOU

It is my prayer that you make bold declaration of every good and perfect gift that comes from God.

Now let me Pray for you:

It is written

"And for me, that utterance may be given unto me, that I may open my mouth boldly, to make known the mystery of the gospel." **Ephesians6:19**

My Father, My Father, Grant me utterance to speak boldly the remaining days of my life, in the Mighty Name of Jesus Christ.

THE POWER OF EVANGELISM

"Go ye therefore, and teach all nations, baptizing them in the name of the Father, and of the Son, and of the Holy Ghost:" **Mathew28:19**

Evangelism has power to attract the blessing of the Lord upon our lives. It is written "And ye shall serve the Lord your God, and he shall bless thy bread, and thy

Chapter 3 : Prayer of Salvation

water; and I will take sickness away from the midst of thee." **Exodus23:26.**

Evangelizing, and bringing men and women to the cross of Jesus Christ is a great commandment. According to the above scripture, we are commanded to teach all nations, the name of Jesus Christ.

It is my prayer that you will witness the name of Jesus Christ to someone today.

Remember………

"And they that be wise shall shine as the brightness of the firmament; and they that turn many to righteousness as the stars for ever and ever." **Daniel12:3**

OPERATION--"ONE MAN TEN MEN"

"Thus saith the Lord of hosts; In those days it shall come to pass, that ten men shall take hold out of all languages of the nations,

even shall take hold of the skirt of him that is a Jew, saying, We will go with you: for we have heard that God is with you."
Zacharia 8:23

If someone directed you to this ministry, it is divine wisdom for you to bring someone else also. If you googled to come into contact with us, I will recommend you also tell ten of your contacts and share with them what Jesus is doing through this ministry. Tell everybody about Jesus, also tell them to contact this ministry. Jesus is Lord!!

OPERATION ONE MAN ONE SOUL

If you cannot bring ten people at one time, at least you can talk to one person per time.

I recommend that you look for just one person who will respond positively and

Chapter 3 : Prayer of Salvation

bring them to church. Or tell them about this ministry. That convert, is your own convert minister to them the love of Jesus Christ.

JESUS IS LORD!

CHAPTER 4
ABOUT THE AUTHOR

Rev Franklin N Abazie is the founding and Presiding Pastor of Miracle of God Ministries with headquarters in Newark, New Jersey USA and a branch church in Owerri-Imo State Nigeria. He is following the footsteps of one of his mentors, Oral Roberts (Healing Evangelist) of the blessed memory. The Lord passed Oral Roberts healing mantle two days before he went to be with the Lord at age 91 into the hand of healing evangelist-Rev Franklin N Abazie in a vision.

In all his services the Power and Presence of God is present to heal all in his audience. He is an ordained man of God with a Healing Ministry reviving the healing and miracle ministry of Jesus Christ of Nazareth.

Pastor Franklin N Abazie, is called by God with a unique mandate: **"THE**

Chapter 4 : About The Author

MOMENT IS DUE TO IMPACT YOUR WORLD THROUGH THE REVIVAL OF THE HEALING & MIRACLE MINISTRY OF JESUS CHRIST OF NAZARETH

I AM SENDING YOU TO RESTORE HEALTH UNTO THEE AND I WILL HEAL THEE OF THY WOUNDS. SAID THE LORD OF HOST"

He is a gifted ardent Teacher of the word of God who operates also in the office of a Prophet, generating and attracting undeniable signs & wonders, special miracles and healings, with apostolic fireworks of the Holy Ghost. He is the founding and presiding senior Pastor of this fast growing Healing ministry. He has written over 86 inspirational, healing and transforming books covering almost all aspect of divine healing and life. He is happily married and blessed with children.

BOOKS BY REV FRANKLIN N ABAZIE

1) Commanding Abundance
2) The outcome of faith
3) Understanding the secret of prevailing prayers.
4) Understanding the secret of the man God uses
5) Activating my due Season
6) Overcoming Divine Verdicts
7) The Outcome of Divine Wisdom
8) Understanding God's Restoration Mandate
9) Walking in the Victory and Authority of the truth
10) Gods Covenant Exemption
11) Destiny Restoration Pillars

Books by Rev Franklin N Abazie

12) Provoking Acceptable Praise
13) Understanding Divine Judgment
14) Activating Angelic Re-enforcement
15) Provoking Un-Merited Favor
16) The Benefits of the Speaking faith
17) Understanding Divine Arrangement
18) Understanding Divine Healing
19) The Mystery of Endurance
20) Obeying Divine Instructions
21) Understanding the Voice of God
22) Never give up on Hope
23) The prevailing Power of faith
24) Understanding Divine Prosperity
25) The Reward of Prayer
26) Covenant Keys to Answered Prayers
27) Activating the Forces of Vengeance

28) Put your faith to work
29) Where is your trust?
30) The Audacity of the Blood of Jesus
31) Redeeming Your Days
32) The Force of Vision
33) Breaking the shackles of Family curses
34) Wisdom for Marriage Stability
35) Overcoming prevailing challenges
36) The Prayer solution
39) The power of Prayer
40) Effective strategy of prayer
41) The prayer that works
42) Walking in Forgiveness
43) The Power of the grace of God
44) The Power of Persistence
45) Overcoming Divine verdicts

46) The benefit of the speaking faith.
47) Fearless faith
48) Redeeming Your Days.
49) The Supernatural Power of Prophecy
50) The companionship of the Holy Spirit
51) Understanding Divine Judgement
52) Understanding Divine Prosperity
53) Dominating Controlling Forces
54) The winner's Faith
55) Destiny Restoration Pillars
56) Developing Spiritual Muscles
57) Inexplicable faith
58) The lifestyle of Prayer
59) Developing a positive attitude in life.
60) The Mystery of Divine supply
61) Encounter with the Power of God

62) Walking in love
63) Praying in the Spirit
64) How to provoke your testimony
65) Walking in the reality of the anointing
66) The Reality of new birth
67) The Price of freedom
68) The Supernatural Power of faith
69) The intellectual components of Redemption.
70) Overcoming Fear
71) Overcoming Prevailing Challenges
72) My life & Ministry
73) The Mystery of Praise

MIRACLE OF GOD MINISTRIES

NIGERIA CRUSADE
2012

MIRACLE OF GOD MINISTRIES

NIGERIA CRUSADE 2012

MIRACLE OF GOD MINISTRIES

*NIGERIA CRUSADE
2012*

¹ But now thus saith the LORD that created thee, O Jacob, and he that formed thee, O Israel, Fear not: for I have redeemed thee, I have called thee by thy name; thou art mine.

Isaiah 43:1

www.ingramcontent.com/pod-product-compliance
Lightning Source LLC
Chambersburg PA
CBHW030123100526
44591CB00009B/503